Contemporary Curved

Jenny Pedigo & Helen Robinson

Landauer Publishing, LLC

Contemporary Curved Quilts

Copyright © 2014 by Landauer Publishing, LLC
Projects Copyright © 2014
by Jenny Pedigo and Helen Robinson
for Sew Kind of Wonderful

This book was designed, produced,
and published by Landauer Publishing, LLC
3100 100th Street, Urbandale, IA 50322
515/287/2144   800/557/2144   landauerpub.com

President/Publisher: Jeramy Lanigan Landauer
Vice President of Sales and Administration: Kitty Jacobson
Editor: Jeri Simon
Art Director: Laurel Albright
Designer, Contemporary Curved Quilts: Lyne Neymeyer
Technical Illustrator: Janet Pittman
Photographer: Sue Voegtlin

ISBN 13: 978-1-935726-61-6

This book printed on acid-free paper.
Printed in United States

10-9-8-7-6-5-4-3

Landauer Books are distributed to the Trade by:
Fox Chapel Publishing
1970 Broad Street
East Petersburg, PA 17520
www.foxchapelpublishing.com
1-800-457-9112

For consumer orders:
Landauer Publishing, LLC
3100 100th Street
Urbandale, Iowa 50322
www.landauerpub.com
1-800-557-2144

Contents

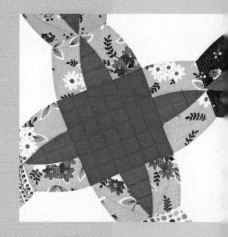

Introduction

"Contemporary Curved Quilts" was inspired by our favorite places to use quilts in our homes. We hope you will enjoy selecting fabrics, colors and texture that will bring a fresh contemporary feel to your favorite spaces.

This book is filled with eight fun quilt projects with a curvy flair as well as instructions on how to use the Quick Curve Ruler© (QCR).

A variety of designs ranging from table toppers to bed quilts can be found in the book. The QCR provides each project with a fun and simple approach to sewing curves with no templates or pinning.

You will need the Quick Curve Ruler© to complete the projects in this book.

Sisters Jenny Pedgio and Helen Robinson began playing with curved quilt designs three years ago. After years of traditional quilting, they wanted to create new, fresh, and contemporary designs that were also easy to piece. The Quick Curve Ruler© was created with simplicity in mind. Since the first Quick Curve Ruler was sold, quilters all over the world have discovered how easy and fun it is to sew curves. Jenny and Helen have a love for combining the newest design trends, whether color

Jenny   Helen

combinations or fabric choices, to create patterns that are fun and contemporary.

Jenny and Helen are ten years apart in age and 1465 miles apart in location. Between them they have 11 children, two husbands, two long-arm machines, several sewing machines, and a crazy obsession for quilting.

Jenny Pedigo & Helen Robinson

Look for the Quick Curve Ruler© at your favorite quilt shop or visit Sewkindofwonderful.com for ordering information and ruler tutorials.

Techniques Quick Curve Ruler© (QCR)

CUTTING THE CURVES

Each project in the book will have its own specific set of Cutting the Curves instructions. We suggest you practice cutting and piecing the curves using the steps provided before beginning a project.

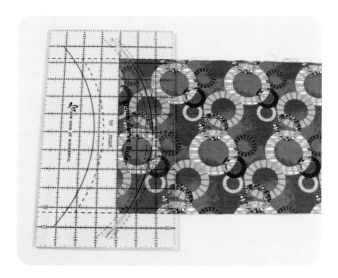

1. Cut (1) 8-½" x width of fabric print strip and (8) 3-½" x 8-½" solid rectangles. This will give you enough pieces to practice making the blocks.

2. Lay the 8-½" x WOF print strip on a cutting mat with the fabric fold on the left. Position the QCR over the left side of the strip centering the top and bottom of the strip between the 1-¾" and 10-¼" dashed lines. The ruler's curve cut out should be close to the left edge but still over the fabric.

3. Using a 45mm rotary cutter, cut in the ruler's curve cut out.

4. Discard the cut fold.

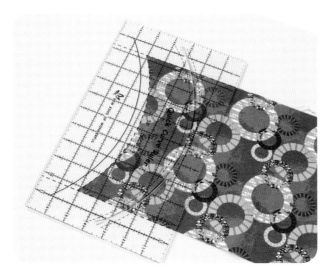

5. Shift the ruler to the right aligning the first curved cut with the ruler's dashed curved line. The top and bottom of the strip should still be centered between the 1-¾" and 10-¼" dashed lines. When the ruler and fabric are aligned, cut in the ruler's curve cut out to create two curve shapes.

6. Continue moving the ruler to the right and aligning the curves to cut additional shapes.

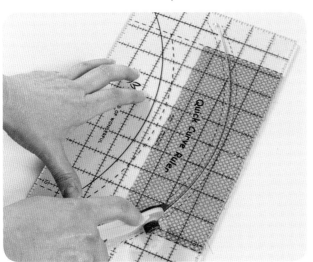

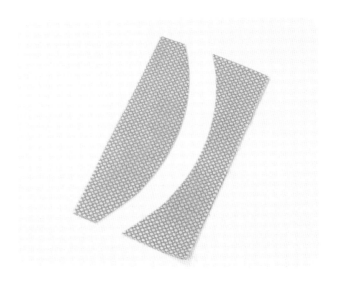

7. Stack a few 3-½" x 8-½" solid rectangles together. Position the QCR on the strips centering the top and bottom of the strips between the 1-¾" and 10-¼" dashed lines. The right edge of the ruler should be aligned with the right edge of the fabric.

8. Using a 45mm rotary cutter, cut in ruler's curve cut out.

9. You will have two different shapes. These are referred to as background shapes A and B.

TIP: Do not stack more than two folded strips when cutting.

PIECING THE CURVES

The curves will be pieced in the same manner in each project. Always use a ¼" seam and sew with right sides together.

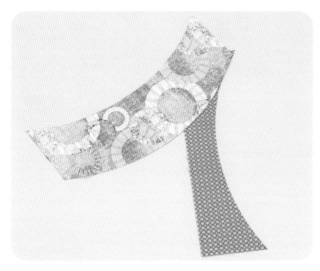

1. Position a print curve shape on a B background shape, right sides together. Extend ¼" of B beyond the print curve.

2. Hold one shape in each hand and slowly bring the curved edges together while stitching a ¼" seam.

TIP: When sewing the curves, I find it easiest to always have the outside curve (top piece) in my right hand and the inside curve (bottom piece) in my left hand. Experiment to see what works best for you.

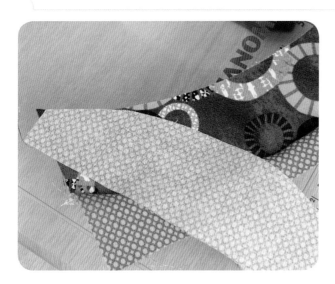

3. Position an A background shape on the piece made in step 2, right sides together. Extend ¼" of the step 2 piece beyond the A background shape. Sew the pieces together as before.

4. Press the seams from the back of the block toward the center curve. Turn the block over and press on the front. You do not need to clip the curves.

SQUARING UP THE SHAPES

Each project in the book will have its own specific set of Squaring up the Shapes instructions. We suggest you practice squaring up the blocks made in Piecing the Curves on page 8 to practice.

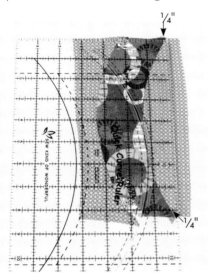

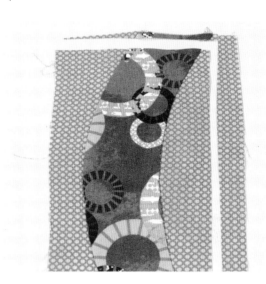

1. Square up the blocks made in Piecing the Curves to 4" x 8" rectangles. Position the QCR on a block with the ¼" marks centered on, or close to, the edges of the piece curve.

2. Trim the right and top edges of the block.

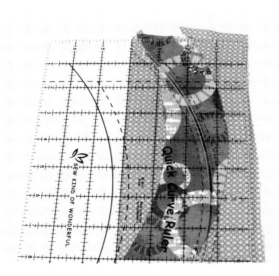

3. Lift the ruler and rotate the block 180-degrees. Reposition the QCR on the block to square it to 4" x 8".

4. Trim the right and top edges to square up the block.

Finished size: 18" x 24"

Crazy Eights Pillow

MATERIALS
(6) 8" x 10" pieces assorted navy fabric
(12) 2-¾" x 10" pieces assorted gold fabric
⅓ yard white fabric
¾ yard backing fabric
¼ yard binding fabric
Standard bed pillow
Quick Curve Ruler© (QCR)

GENERAL CUTTING INSTRUCTIONS

 From assorted navy fabric, cut:
(6) 8″ x 10″ pieces.

 From assorted gold fabric, cut:
(12) 2-¾″ x 10″ pieces.

From white fabric, cut:
(4) 3-½" x WOF strips.
   From the strips, cut: (12) 3-½" x 10" pieces

 From backing fabric, cut:
(2) 17" x 19" backing pieces

 From binding fabric, cut:
(3) 2-½" x WOF binding strips

WOF = width of fabric
Read through Using the Quick Curve Ruler© on
pages 6-9 before beginning this project.

CUTTING THE CURVES

1. Stack a few 8" x 10" assorted navy pieces together, right sides up. Position the QCR on the pieces centering the top and bottom of the pieces between the 1" and 11" lines. The left side of the fabric should be on the 3-½" mark as shown. Using a rotary cutter, cut in the ruler's curve cut out.

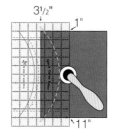

2. Reposition the QCR with the 5" mark on the curved points. Cut in the ruler's curve cut out to make N shapes. Continue cutting N shapes in the same manner cutting 2 from each assorted navy piece for a total of 12 N shapes.

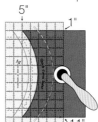

Cut 12 N shapes

3. Cut (6) 1-¾" x 9-1/2" C rectangles using the leftover assorted navy pieces.

Cut 6
C rectangles

4. Stack a few 2-¾" x 10" assorted gold pieces together, right sides up. Position the QCR on the pieces centering the top and bottom of the pieces between the 1" and 11" lines. Cut in the ruler's curve cut out to make G shapes. Discard the small pieces. Make 12 G shapes.

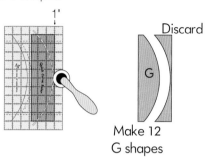

Make 12
G shapes

5. Stack a few 3-½" x 10" white pieces together, right sides up. Position the QCR on the pieces centering the top and bottom of the pieces between the 1" and 11" lines. The left side of the fabric should be on the 3-⅛" mark as shown. Cut in the ruler's curve cut out to make W shapes. Discard the small pieces. Make 12 W shapes.

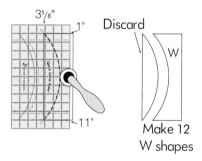

Make 12
W shapes

PIECING THE CURVES

1. Referring to the diagram, position a G shape on an N shape, right sides together, with a ¼" of N extending beyond G as shown.

2. Hold one shape in each hand and slowly bring the curved edges together while stitching a ¼" seam. Press seams toward N to make an NG shape. Make 12 NG shapes.

Make 12 NG shapes

3. Referring to the diagram, position an NG shape on a W shape, right sides together, with a ¼" of W extending beyond NG as shown. Hold one shape in each hand and slowly bring the curved edges together while stitching a ¼" seam. Press seams toward N to make a WNG shape. Make 12 WNG shapes.

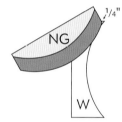

Make 12
WNG shapes

SQUARING UP THE SHAPES

Square up the WNG shapes to 4" x 9-½". Position the QCR on a WNG shape with the ¼" mark on the curved seam in the corners as shown. Trim the right and top edges of the shape. Lift the ruler and rotate the fabric 180-degrees. Reposition the QCR on the shape so the previously trimmed edges are now on the ¼" marks. Trim the right and top edges. Repeat with the remaining WNG shapes.

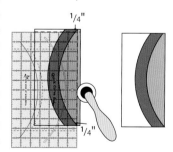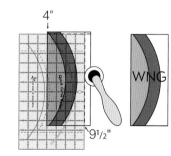

MAKING THE BLOCKS

Randomly select 2 WNG shapes and 1 C shape as shown. Sew the pieces together and press the seams toward the C shape to make a block. Make 6 blocks.

Make 6 blocks

MAKING THE PILLOW TOP

1. Referring to the diagram, lay out the blocks in 2 rows with 3 blocks in each row.

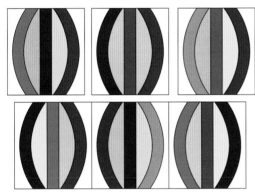

Pillow Front Diagram

2. Sew the blocks together in rows. Press the seams. Sew the rows together to complete the pillow top.

3. Quilt the pillow top as desired.

PILLOW ASSEMBLY

1. Hem a $\frac{1}{4}$" rolled hem on one 19" side of each of the backing pieces.

2. Lay the quilted pillow top right side down and position a backing piece right side up with the hemmed edge toward the center. The top, bottom and left edges should be aligned with the pillow top underneath.

3. In the same manner, layer the remaining backing piece on the pillow top with the top, bottom and right edges aligned with the pillow top underneath. The center hemmed edges should overlap 3"-4" or more.

4. Pin the layers together on all sides. Stitch a $\frac{1}{4}$" seam around the entire pillow. Trim any extra fabric even with the quilted pillow top.

5. Sew the (3) 2-$\frac{1}{2}$" x WOF binding strips together to make one continuous strip. Press the strip in half lengthwise, wrong sides together, and sew to the raw edge of the pillow. Fold over raw edges and hand stitch in place on back of pillow.

Finished size: 21" x 81"

Midnight Mosaic Runner

MATERIALS

1-⅓ yards gray fabric
1-⅓ yards white fabric
⅔ yard navy fabric
½ yard binding fabric
Quick Curve Ruler© (QCR)
10" or larger square-up ruler

GENERAL CUTTING INSTRUCTIONS

From gray fabric, cut:
(16) 10" squares

From white fabric, cut:
(2) 10" x WOF strips.
    From the strips, cut: (28) 3" x 10" pieces.
(1) 3" x WOF strip.
    From the strip, cut: (4) 3" x 10" pieces
(11) 1-½" x WOF strips.
    From 4 of the strips, cut:
    (14) 1-½" x 9-½" rectangles
    Set aside the remaining 1-½" strips for
    sashing and borders.

From the navy fabric, cut:
(3) 7" x WOF strips.
    From the strips, cut: (16) 7" squares.

From binding fabric, cut:
(6) 2-½" x WOF strips.

WOF = width of fabric
Read through Using the Quick Curve Ruler®
on pages 6-9 before beginning this project.

CUTTING THE CURVES AND MAKING THE BLOCKS

1. Stack a few 10" gray squares together, right sides up, and cut in half diagonally.

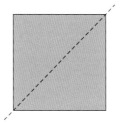
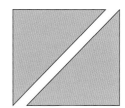

2. Position the QCR over the triangle as shown. Align the left edge of the triangle with the 2-¾" vertical marks on the QCR. The top and bottom right sides of the triangle should be on the 1-¾" marks of the QCR.

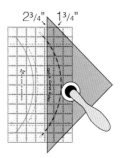

3. Cut in the ruler's curve cut out to make an A piece. Repeat with the remaining 10" gray squares to make 32 A pieces.

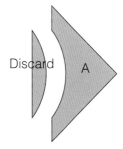

Make 32 A piece

4. Stack a few 3" x 10" white pieces together, right sides up. Referring to the diagram, position the QCR on the pieces centering the top and bottom of the pieces between the 1" and 11" lines. The right edge of the fabric should be under the 1" vertical

line. Cut in the ruler's curve cut out to make a B piece. Repeat with the remaining 3" x 10" white pieces to make 32 B pieces.

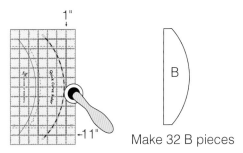

Make 32 B pieces

5. Stack a couple 7" navy squares together, right sides up, and cut in half diagonally.

6. Position the QCR over the triangle as shown. Align the left edge of the triangle with the 2-½" vertical marks on the QCR. The top and bottom points of the triangle should be centered between the 1" and 11" lines. Cut in the ruler's curve cut out to make a C piece. Make 1" marks from each point. Repeat with the remaining 7" navy squares to make 32 C pieces.

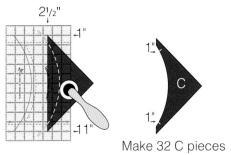

Make 32 C pieces

PIECING THE CURVES

1. Referring to the diagram, position a B piece on top of an A piece, right sides together. Extend the B curved end ⅛" past the A piece.

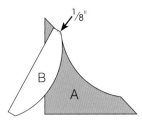

2. Begin sewing the pieces together with a ¼" seam, easing the two bias edges together as you sew. Press to make an AB triangle. Make 32 AB triangles. Place the QCR on the long edge of an AB triangle. Cut off any excess B fabric to square up the side. Repeat with the remaining AB triangles.

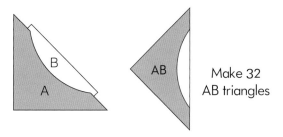

Make 32 AB triangles

3. Sew pairs of AB triangles together as shown to make a D unit. Press seams open. Make 16 D units.

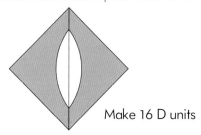

Make 16 D units

4. Position the QCR on a D unit with the corner centered between the 4-½" and 7-½" marks on the ruler. The center seam should be at the ruler's 5-¼" vertical marks. Cut in the ruler's curve cut out. Lift the QCR, rotate it 180-degrees, and cut the curve on the opposite side of the D unit. Referring to the diagram, mark the units where the curve and straight edges meet. Repeat with the remaining D units.

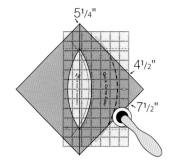 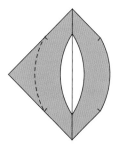

5. Matching the marks, position a D unit on a C piece, right sides together, with 1" of C extending beyond D to create the seam allowance as shown. Begin sewing the pieces together using a ¼" seam and easing the two bias edges together as you sew. In the same manner, sew another C piece to the opposite side of the D unit. Press both ends to make a block. Make 16 blocks.

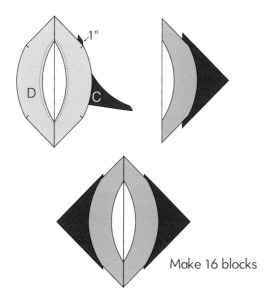

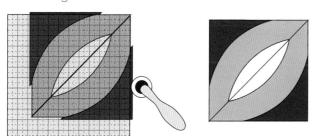

Make 16 blocks

SQUARING UP THE BLOCKS

Using a 10" or larger square-up ruler, square the blocks to 9-½". Position the diagonal line of the square-up ruler over the center seam of the block. Center the block equally within the 9-½" square. Cut off excess fabric on all sides of block. Square up the remaining blocks.

RUNNER ASSEMBLY

1. Referring to the Runner Assembly Diagram, lay out the 16 blocks and 1-½" x 9-½" white rectangles in 2 rows as shown.

2. Sew the white rectangles and blocks together in each row to make 2 rows.

3. Measure the length of a row and cut (3) 1-½" x WOF white strips to this measurement. Pin and sew the strips to the block rows as shown. Press seams toward the strips.

4. Measure the width of the piece sewn in step 3. Cut (2) 1-½" x WOF strips to this measurement. Sew the strips to opposite edges of the piece to complete the runner top. Press.

Runner Assembly Diagram

FINISHING THE RUNNER

1. Layer the runner top, batting and backing together. Quilt as desired.

2. Sew the (6) 2-½" x WOF binding strips together to make one continuous strip. Press the strip in half lengthwise and sew the binding strip to the raw edge of the runner top. Fold over raw edges and hand stitch in place on back of the runner.

Finished size: 72" x 96"

Fresh and Trendy Quilt

MATERIALS

½ yard each of 6 assorted orange print fabrics
½ yard each of 6 assorted blue print fabrics
¼ yard each of 6 assorted green print fabrics
4 yards white fabric
3-¼ yards gray fabric
⅔ yard binding fabric
5 yards backing
Queen-size batting
Quick Curve Ruler© (QCR)

GENERAL CUTTING INSTRUCTIONS

From each assorted orange print fabric, cut:
(2) 7" x WOF strips. From each strip, cut:
　(2) 7" x 12" pieces for a total of 24 pieces.

From each assorted blue print fabric, cut:
(2) 8" x WOF strips. From each strip, cut:
　(4) 8" squares for a total of 48 squares.

From each assorted green print fabric, cut:
(8) 4" squares for a total of 48 squares.

From the white fabric, cut:

(10) 8" x WOF strips. From each strip, cut:
　(5) 8" squares for a total of 50 squares.
　You will use 48.
(8) 6-½"x WOF strips. From each strip, cut:
　(6) 6-½" squares for a total of 48 squares.

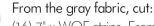

From the gray fabric, cut:
(16) 7" x WOF strips. From each strip, cut:
　(3) 7" x 12" pieces for a total of 48 pieces.

From binding fabric, cut:
(9) 2-½" binding strips

WOF = width of fabric
Read through *Using the Quick Curve Ruler©*
on pages 6-9 before beginning this project.

CUTTING THE CURVES

1. Stack a few 7" x 12" orange and gray pieces together, right sides up. Measure and mark 7" on each long edge as shown. Position the QCR on the fabric with the ruler's curve cut out on the 7" mark and opposite corner. Cut in the curve cut out to make an A piece.

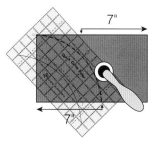

2. In the same manner, position the QCR on the remaining 7" mark and cut to make another A piece. Discard small piece in center. Repeat with the remaining 7" x 12" pieces to make 48 assorted orange A pieces and 96 gray A pieces.

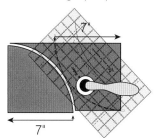

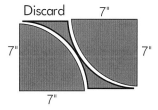

Cut 48 assorted
orange A

Cut 96 gray A

3. Cut the 8" blue and white squares in half diagonally.

4. Stack a few blue and white triangles together, right sides up. Measure in ½" on both points and trim.

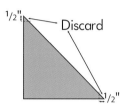

5. Position the QCR on the triangles with the ruler's curve cut out over the points as shown. Cut in the curve cut out to make B pieces. Discard the small pieces.

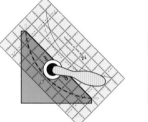

6. Repeat with the remaining blue and white triangles to make 48 white B pieces and 96 blue B pieces

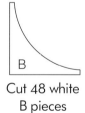 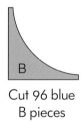

Cut 48 white
B pieces

Cut 96 blue
B pieces

PIECING THE CURVES

1. Separate the gray A pieces and blue B pieces into one set and the orange A pieces and white B pieces into another.

2. Referring to the diagram, position a gray A piece on a blue B piece, right sides together, with a ½" tail of B showing. Hold one piece in each hand and slowly bring the curved edges together while stitching a ¼" seam. Press the seams toward the blue B piece to make an AB gray/blue set. Make 96 AB gray/blue sets.

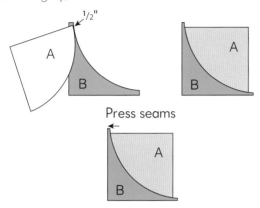

Press seams

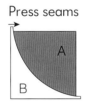

Make 96 gray/blue
AB sets

3. In the same manner, sew the orange A and white B pieces together. Press the seams toward the orange A piece to make an AB white/orange set. Make 48 AB white/orange sets.

Press seams

Make 48 white/orange
AB sets

4. Draw a diagonal line on the wrong side of the 4" assorted green squares.

5. Position a marked 4" assorted green square on the bottom right corner of a 6-½" white square as shown, right sides together.

6. Stitch on the drawn line. Trim the corner fabric a ¼" past the stitched line. Press the green triangle open and the seam toward the green fabric to make a white/green diamond set. Make 48 white/green diamond sets.

Make 48 white/green
diamond sets

SQUARING UP THE AB SETS

Square up the AB sets to 6-½". Position the QCR on an AB set with the 6-½" mark on the curved seam in the corners as shown. Trim the right and top edges of the set. Lift the ruler and rotate the AB set 180-degrees. Reposition the QCR on the shape so the previously trimmed edges are now on the 6-½" vertical and horizontal lines. Trim the right and top edges. Repeat with the remaining AB sets.

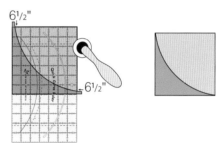

MAKING THE BLOCKS

1. Lay out 4 AB white/orange sets as shown. Sew the sets right sides together in rows. Sew the rows together to make an orange/white circle. Press all seams open to reduce bulk. Make 12 white/orange circles.

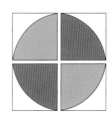 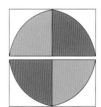 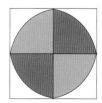

Make 12
white/orange circles

2. Lay out 2 AB gray/blue sets as shown. Sew the sets right side together with a ¼" seam to make an AB gray/blue pair. Press seams open to reduce bulk. Make 48 AB gray/blue pairs.

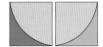

Make 48 AB
gray/blue pairs

3. Lay out an orange/white circle, 4 AB gray/blue pairs and 4 white/green diamond sets as shown.

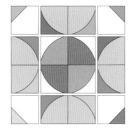

4. Sew the pieces together in rows. Sew the rows together to make a block. Press all seams open to reduce bulk. Make 12 blocks.

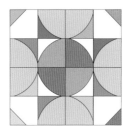

Make 12 blocks

QUILT ASSEMBLY

1. Referring to the Quilt Assembly Diagram, lay out the blocks in 4 rows with 3 blocks in each row.

2. Sew the blocks together in rows. Press the seam. Sew the rows together to complete the quilt top. Press.

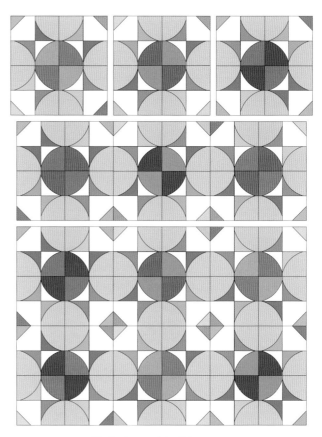

Quilt Assembly Diagram

FINISHING THE QUILT

1. Layer the quilt top, batting and backing together. Quilt as desired.

2. Sew the (9) 2-½" x WOF binding strips together to make one continuous strip. Press the strip in half lengthwise and sew the binding strip to the raw edge of the quilt top. Fold over raw edges and hand stitch in place on back of quilt.

Finished size: 60" x 80"

Modern Millie Quilt

MATERIALS
3-$\frac{1}{2}$ yards taupe print fabric
8 assorted black and white fat quarters
$\frac{1}{3}$ yard golden yellow fabric
$\frac{1}{2}$ yard binding fabric
5 yards backing fabric
Twin-size batting
Quick Curve Ruler© (QCR)

GENERAL CUTTING INSTRUCTIONS

From taupe print fabric, cut:
(6) 10-$\frac{1}{2}$" x WOF strips. From the strips, cut:
    (24) 10-$\frac{1}{2}$" squares
(8) 7" x WOF strips. From the strips, cut:
    (48) 7" squares. Cut each 7" square
    in half diagonally for a total of
    96 half-square triangles.

From each assorted black and white fat quarter, cut:
(6) 6" x 10" pieces

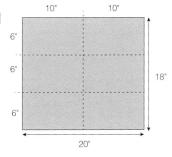

From golden yellow fabric, cut:
(5) 2" x WOF strips. From the strips, cut:
    (96) 2" squares

From binding fabric, cut:
(8) 2-$\frac{1}{2}$" binding strips

WOF = width of fabric
Read through Using the Quick Curve Ruler®
on pages 6-9 before beginning this project.

CUTTING THE CURVES

1. Stack a few 7" taupe print half-square triangles, right sides up. Measure in $\frac{1}{2}$" on both points and trim as shown.

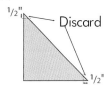

2. Position the QCR so the curve cut out lays over the points as shown. Using a rotary cutter, cut in the ruler's curve cut out to make an A shape. Discard the small section. Repeat with the remaining half-square triangles to make 96 A shapes.

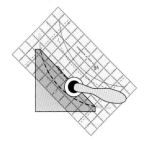

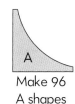

Make 96
A shapes

3. Stack a few 6" x 10" black and white pieces, right sides up. Measure and mark 6" on each long edge as shown.

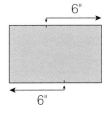

4. Position the QCR on the fabric with the ruler's curve cut out on the 6" mark and opposite corner. Cut in the curve cut out to make a B shape.

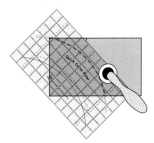
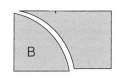

5. In the same manner, position the QCR on the remaining 6" mark and cut to make another B shape. Discard small piece in center. Repeat with the remaining 6" x 10" black and white pieces to make 96 B shapes.

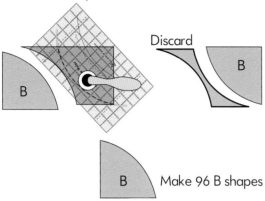

Discard

Make 96 B shapes

PIECING THE CURVES

1. Referring to the diagram, position a B shape on an A shape, right sides together, with a ½" of A extending beyond B.

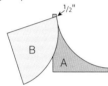

2. Hold one shape in each hand and slowly bring the curved edges together while stitching a 1/4" seam. Press seams toward B to make an AB shape. Press the shape from the front and back. Make 96 AB shapes.

Press seams

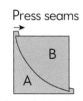

Make 96 AB shapes

SQUARING UP THE SHAPES

Square up the AB shapes to 5-½". Position the QCR on an AB shape with the 5-½" mark on the curved seam in the corners as shown. Trim the right and top edges of the shape. Lift the ruler and rotate the fabric 180-degrees. Reposition the QCR on the shape so the previously trimmed edges are now on the 5-½" vertical and horizontal lines. Trim the right and top edges. Repeat with the remaining AB shapes.

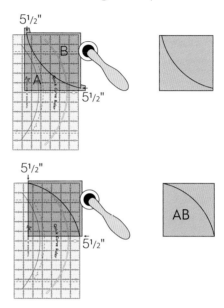

MAKING THE BLOCKS

1. Draw a diagonal line on the wrong side of all the 2" squares.

2. Position a 2" square on the bottom right corner of an AB shape as shown, right sides together. Stitch on the drawn line. Trim the corner fabric a ¼" past the stitched line. Press fabric open to make an AB unit. Make 96 AB units.

Make 96 AB units

3. Lay out 4 matching AB units as shown. The fabric in the 4 AB units should be the same.

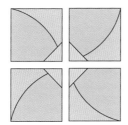

4. Sew the units together in rows. Sew the rows together to make a block. Press the seams open to reduce bulk. The block should measure 10-½" square. Make 24 blocks.

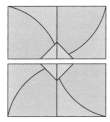
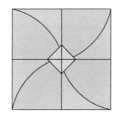

Make 24 blocks

QUILT ASSEMBLY

1. Referring to the Quilt Assembly Diagram, lay out the blocks and 10-½" taupe print squares, alternating the blocks and squares in each row.

2. Sew the pieces together in rows. Press the seams. Sew the rows together to complete the quilt top. Press.

Quilt Assembly Diagram

FINISHING THE QUILT

1. Layer the quilt top, batting and backing together. Quilt as desired.

2. Sew the (8) 2-½" x WOF binding strips together to make one continuous strip. Press the strip in half lengthwise and sew the binding strip to the raw edge of the quilt top. Fold over raw edges and hand stitch in place on back of quilt.

Finished size: 63" x 80"

Tulip Festival Quilt

MATERIALS

5-½" x 20" piece each of 15 assorted floral fabrics
¼ yard each of 5 assorted white print fabrics
⅓ yard solid green fabric
½ yard solid white fabric
4-¾ yards background fabric
    Note: Fabric from Michael Miller Essex line;
    100% cotton natural color linen
⅔ yard binding fabric
5 yards backing fabric
Quick Curve Ruler© (QCR)
10" or larger square-up ruler

GENERAL CUTTING INSTRUCTIONS

From each assorted floral fabric, cut:
(2) 5-½" x 10" pieces for tulips

From each assorted white print fabric, cut:
(3) 7-½" x 10" pieces for vases

From solid green fabric, cut:
(3) 1-½" x WOF strips. From 1 strip, cut:
    (2) 1-½" x 20" strips. Set 1 aside.

From solid white fabric, cut:
(8) 1-1/2" x WOF strips for outer border

From background fabric, cut:
(4) 10" x WOF strips. From the strips, cut:
    (30) 4-¼" x 10" pieces for vase sides
(5) 4-½" x WOF strips. From 1 strip, cut:
    (2) 4-½" x 20" strips.
(5) 6-½" x WOF strips. From the strips, cut:
    (30) 6-½" squares.
    Cut each square in half
    diagonally for a total of
    60 half-square triangles.
(1) 23" x WOF strip. From the strip, cut:
    (12) 2-½" x 23" block sashing strips.
(18) 2-½" x WOF strips for row sashing and
    borders

From binding fabric, cut:
(8) 2-½" x WOF binding strips

WOF = width of fabric
Read through Using the Quick Curve Ruler©
on pages 6-9 before beginning this project.

CUTTING THE CURVES

1. Stack a few 5-$\frac{1}{2}$" x 10" floral pieces, right sides up. Measure and mark 5-$\frac{1}{2}$" on each long edge as shown.

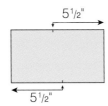

2. Position the QCR on the fabric with the ruler's curve cut out on the 5-$\frac{1}{2}$" mark and opposite corner. Cut in the curve cut out to make B shapes.

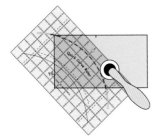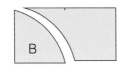

3. In the same manner, position the QCR on the remaining 5-$\frac{1}{2}$" mark and cut to make another B shape. Discard fabric piece in center. Repeat with the remaining 5-$\frac{1}{2}$" x 10" floral pieces to make a total of 60 B shapes.

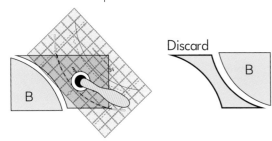

4. Stack a few 6-$\frac{1}{2}$" background half-square triangles, right sides up. Measure in $\frac{1}{2}$" on both points and trim as shown.

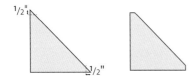

5. Position the QCR so the curve cut out lays over the points as shown. Using a rotary cutter, cut in the ruler's curve cut out to make A shapes. Discard the small section. Repeat with the remaining half-square triangles to make a total of 60 A shapes.

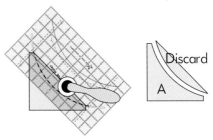

6. Stack a few 7-$\frac{1}{2}$" x 10" white print pieces vertically, right sides up. Position the QCR on the pieces centering the top and bottom of the pieces between the 1" and 11" lines. The right side of the fabric should be on the 1" vertical line as shown. Using a rotary cutter, cut in the ruler's curve cut out. Discard the small pieces. Lift the ruler and rotate the fabric 180-degrees. Cut the opposite side of the pieces in the same manner to make C shapes. Repeat with the remaining 7-$\frac{1}{2}$" x 10" pieces to make a total of 15 C shapes.

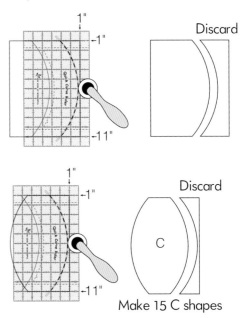

Make 15 C shapes

7. Stack a few 4-$\frac{1}{4}$" x 10" background pieces, right sides up. Position the QCR on the pieces centering the top and bottom of the pieces between the 1" and 11" lines. The left side of the fabric should be on the 3-$\frac{1}{8}$" vertical line as shown. Using a rotary

cutter, cut in the ruler's curve cut out to make a D shape. Discard the small pieces. Repeat with the remaining 4-¼" x 10" background pieces to make a total of 30 D shapes.

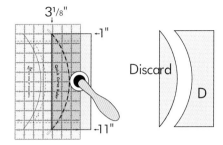

PIECING THE CURVES

1. Referring to the diagram, position a B shape on an A shape, right sides together, with a ½" of A extending beyond B as shown.

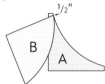

2. Hold one shape in each hand and slowly bring the curved edges together while stitching a ¼" seam. Press seams toward B to make an AB unit. Make 60 AB units.

Make 60 AB units

3. Referring to the diagram, position a C shape on a D shape, right sides together, with a ¼" of D extending beyond C as shown.

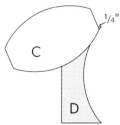

4. Hold one shape in each hand and slowly bring the curved edges together while stitching a ¼" seam.

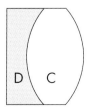

5. In the same manner, sew D to the opposite side of C as shown. Press seams toward C to make a DCD shape. Make 15 DCD units.

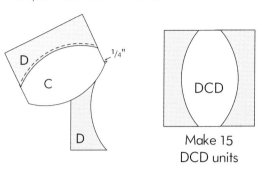

Make 15 DCD units

SQUARING UP THE SHAPES

1. Square up the AB units to 5". Position the QCR on an AB unit with the 5" mark on the curved seam in the corners as shown. Trim the right and top edges of the unit. Lift the ruler and rotate the fabric 180-degrees. Reposition the QCR on the unit so the previously trimmed edges are now on the 5" vertical and horizontal lines. Trim the right and top edges. Repeat with the remaining AB units.

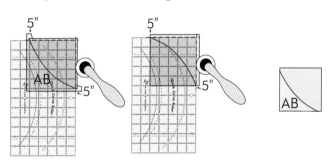

2. Square up the DCD units to 9-½". Position a 10" or larger square-up ruler on DCD. Referring to the diagram, place the 3-1/8" mark at the top of the unit and the 9-½" mark along the bottom edge and trim. Repeat on other remaining side of the unit. Square up the remaining DCD units to 9-½".

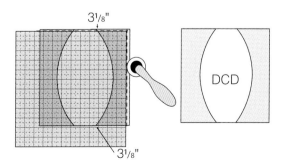

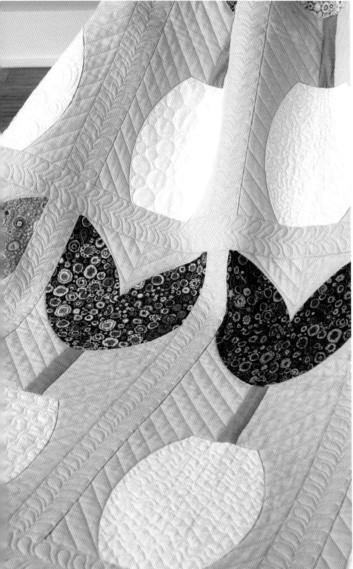

MAKING THE BLOCKS

1. Lay out 4 matching AB units as shown. Sew the units together in rows. Sew the rows together to make a tulip section. Press the seams open to reduce bulk. The section should measure 9-½" square. Make 15 tulip sections.

    Make 15
    tulip sections

2. Lay out (2) 4-½" x WOF background strips and (1) 1-½" x WOF solid green strip as shown. Sew the strips together to make a strip set. Press seams toward green strip. Make 2 strip sets.

    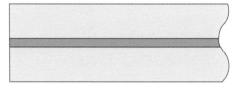

3. In the same manner, sew (2) 4-½" x 20" background strips and (1) 1-½" x 20" solid green strip together to make 1 strip set.

4. Cut the strip sets into 5" segments to make 15 stem sections.

    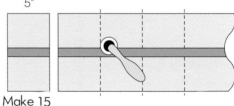

    Make 15
    stem sections

5. Lay out a tulip section, stem section and DCD unit as shown. Sew the pieces together. Press the seams toward the stem section to make a tulip block. Make 15 tulip blocks.

    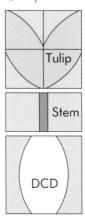 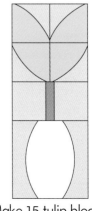

    Make 15 tulip blocks

QUILT ASSEMBLY

1. Lay out 5 tulip blocks and (4) 2-½" x 23" block sashing strips as shown. Sew the pieces together to make a block row. The row should measure 23" x 53-½". Make 3 block rows.

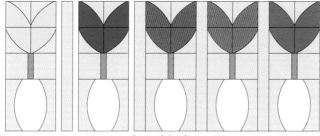

Make 3 block rows

2. Sew the 2-½" x WOF background strips together along the short edges to make one continuous strip. Press the seams open.
Note: Measure the width of each block row; they should measure 53-½". If the rows are not a consistent measurement, take the average of the three to cut the sashing lengths.

3. From the continuous strip in step 2, cut (4) 2-½" x 53-½" row sashing strips and (2) 2-½" x 76" side sashing strips.

4. Referring to the Quilt Assembly Diagram, sew the row sashing strips to the block rows. Press. Sew the side sashing strips to opposite sides of the rows to make the quilt center.

5. Sew the 1-½" x WOF solid white strips together along the short edges to make one continuous strip. From the strip, cut (2) 1-½" x 57-½" top/bottom border strips and (2) 1-½ x 78" side border strips.

6. Sew the white top/bottom border strips to the top and bottom of the quilt center. Press. Sew the white side border strips to the sides of the quilt center. Press.

7. From the remaining 2-½" continuous background strip in step 2, cut (2) 2-½" x 59-½" top/bottom outer border strips and (2) 2-½" x 81" side outer border strips.

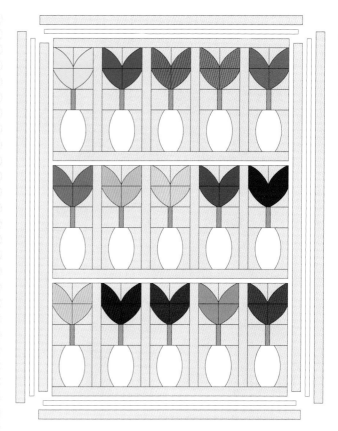

Quilt Assembly Diagram

8. Sew the top/bottom outer border strips to the top and bottom of the quilt center. Press. Sew the side outer border strips to the sides of the quilt center. Press to complete the quilt top.

FINISHING THE QUILT

1. Layer the quilt top, batting and backing together. Quilt as desired.

2. Sew the (8) 2-½" x WOF binding strips together to make one continuous strip. Press the strip in half lengthwise and sew the binding strip to the raw edge of the quilt top. Fold over raw edges and hand stitch in place on back of quilt.

Finished size: 78" x 91"

Sassy Stars Quilt

MATERIALS

½ yard each of 7 assorted print fabrics
   (use more fabrics for a scrappier look)
3-¾ yards solid teal fabric
4-¾ yards solid white fabric
⅔ yard binding
7 yards backing fabric
Double-size batting
Quick Curve Ruler© (QCR)

GENERAL CUTTING INSTRUCTIONS

From each assorted print fabric, cut:
(2) 8-½" x WOF strips

From solid teal fabric, cut:
(9) 8-½" x WOF strips. From the strips, cut:
   (168) 2" x 8-½" pieces
(7) 6-½" x WOF strips. From the strips, cut:
   (42) 6-½" squares

From solid white fabric, cut:
(11) 8-½" x WOF strips. From the strips, cut:
   (168) 2-½" x 8-½"pieces
(17) 4" x WOF strips. From the strips, cut:
   (168) 4" squares

From binding fabric, cut:
(9) 2-½" x WOF binding strips

WOF = width of fabric
Read through Using the Quick Curve Ruler©
on pages 6-9 before beginning this project.

Wood Sculpture on page 34 by Charles Landauer;
photographed with permission.

CUTTING THE CURVES

1. Stack a few 8-½" x WOF printed strips together.
    If the strips are folded, do not stack more than two.
    Position the QCR on the strips centering the top
    and bottom of the strips between the 1-¾" and
    10-¼" dashed lines. The left side of the fabric should
    be on the 3" mark as shown. Using a rotary cutter,
    cut in the ruler's cut out.

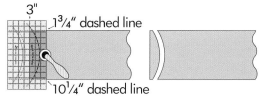

3"
1³/₄" dashed line
10¹/₄" dashed line

2. Shift the ruler to the right aligning the curved cut
    with the ruler's dashed curved line. The top and
    bottom of the fabric should be centered between
    the 1-¾" and 10-¼" marks. Cut in the ruler's curve
    cut out to make A shapes. Continue in the same
    manner to cut additional A shapes. Repeat with the
    remaining 8-½" x WOF print strips to make a total
    of 168 A shapes.

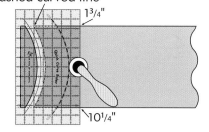

dashed curved line
1³/₄"
10¹/₄"

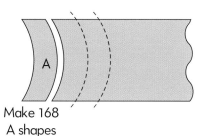

A

Make 168
A shapes

3. Stack a few 2" x 8-½" teal strips together. Position
    the QCR on the strips centering the top and bottom
    of the strips between the 1-¾" and 10-¼" dashed
    lines. The right side of the fabric should be on the

1" mark as shown. Cut in curve cut out to make B shapes. Discard the small piece. Repeat with the remaining 2" x 8-½" teal strips to make a total of 168 B shapes.

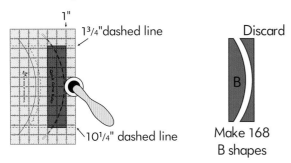

1"

1³/₄"dashed line

10¹/₄" dashed line

Discard

B

Make 168
B shapes

4. Stack a few 2-½" x 8-½" white strips together. Position the QCR on the strips centering the top and bottom of the strips between the 1-³/₄" and 10-¼" dashed lines. The right edge of the ruler should be aligned with the right edge of the fabric as shown. Cut in curve cut out to make a W shape. Discard the small piece. Repeat with the remaining 2-½" x 8-½" white strips to make a total of 168 W shapes.

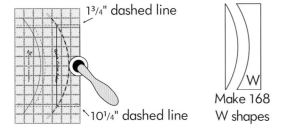

1³/₄" dashed line

10¹/₄" dashed line

W

Make 168
W shapes

PIECING THE CURVES

1. Referring to the diagram, position an A shape on a W shape, right sides together, with ¼" of W extending beyond A.

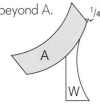

¼"

A

W

2. Hold one shape in each hand and slowly bring the curved edges together while stitching a ¼" seam to make a WA piece. Make 168 WA pieces.

WA

Make 168
WA shapes

3. Referring to the diagram, position a B shape on a WA piece, right sides together, with a ¼" of WA extending beyond B. Hold one shape in each hand and slowly bring the curved edges together while stitching a ¼" seam to make a WAB shape. Press the seams toward the teal. Press the shape from the back and then the front. Make 168 WAB shapes.

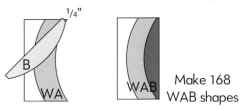

¼"

B

WA

WAB

Make 168
WAB shapes

SQUARING UP THE SHAPES

Square up the WAB shapes to 8" x 3-½". Position the QCR on a WAB shape with the ⅛" mark on the curved seams as shown. Trim the right and top edges of the shape. Lift the ruler and rotate the shape 180-degrees. Reposition the QCR on the shape so the left edge is on the 3-½" mark and the bottom edge is on the 8" line. Trim the right and top edges. Repeat with the remaining WAB shapes.

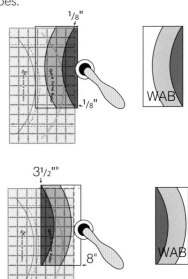

⅛"

⅛"

WAB

3¹/₂""

8"

WAB

MAKING THE BLOCKS

1. Lay out 2 matching WAB shapes as shown. The fabric in the 2 WAB shapes should be the same. Sew the shapes together using a ¼" seam. Press the seam open to make a WAB block. Make 84 matching WAB blocks.

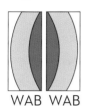

WAB WAB

Make 84
matching WAB blocks

2. Cut the WAB blocks in half as shown to make 168 WAB half blocks.

4"

4"

Make 168
WAB half blocks

3. Lay out 4 matching WAB half blocks, (4) 4" solid white squares and (1) 6-½" teal square as shown. Sew the pieces together in rows. Sew the rows together to make a block. Press all seams open to reduce bulk. The block should measure 13-½" square. Make 42 blocks.

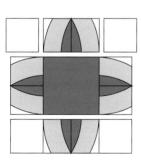
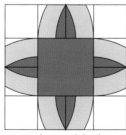

Make 42 blocks

QUILT ASSEMBLY

1. Referring to the Quilt Assembly Diagram, lay out the blocks in 7 rows with 6 blocks in each row.

2. Sew the blocks together in rows. Press the seams. Sew the rows together to complete the quilt top. Press.

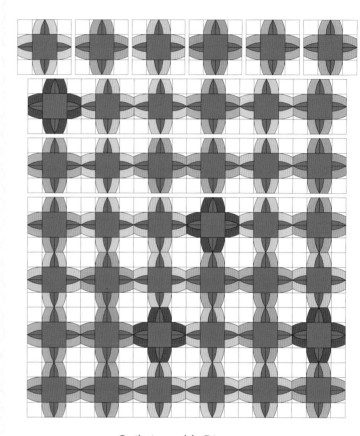

Quilt Assembly Diagram

FINISHING THE QUILT

1. Layer the quilt top, batting and backing together. Quilt as desired.

2. Sew the (9) 2-½" x WOF binding strips together to make one continuous strip. Press the strip in half lengthwise and sew the binding strip to the raw edge of the quilt top. Fold over raw edges and hand stitch in place on back of quilt.

Finished size: 41" x 41"

Argyle Abby Wallhanging

MATERIALS
¾ yard solid aqua fabric
2/3 yard print fabric
1/4 yard white solid
1-1/4 yards solid gray fabric
½ yard binding fabric
1-½ yards backing fabric
Crib-size batting
Quick Curve Ruler© (QCR)
10" or larger square-up ruler

GENERAL CUTTING INSTRUCTIONS

From solid aqua fabric, cut:
(8) 3" x WOF strips

From print fabric, cut:
(6) 3" x WOF strips

From solid white fabric, cut:
(3) 2-½" x WOF strips. From 1 of the strips, cut:
   (1) 2-½" x 20" strip

From solid gray fabric, cut:
(5) 4" x WOF strips. From 1 of the strips, cut:
   (1) 4" x 20" strip
(2) 5" x WOF strips. From the strips, cut:
   (4) 5" squares
   (8) 3" x 5" rectangles
   (4) 3" squares
(1) 10" x WOF strip. From the strip, cut:
   (14) 3" x 10" pieces
(1) 3" x WOF strip. From the strip, cut:
   (4) 3" x 10" pieces

From binding fabric, cut:
(5) 2-½" binding strips

WOF = width of fabric
Read through Using the Quick Curve Ruler©
on pages 6-9 before beginning this project.

CUTTING THE CURVES AND MAKING THE BLOCKS

1. Stack a few 3" x 10" gray pieces together, right sides up. Position the QCR on the pieces centering the top and bottom of the pieces between the 1" and 11" lines. The left side of the fabric should be on the 3-⅛" mark as shown. Using a rotary cutter, cut in the ruler's curve cut out. Discard the small pieces. Repeat with the remaining 3" x 10" gray pieces to make a total of 18 B pieces.

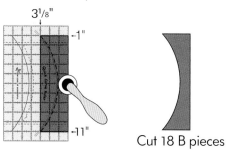

Cut 18 B pieces

2. Lay out (2) 3" x WOF aqua strips and (1) 3" x WOF print strip as shown. Offset the strips by 3" at the top. Sew strips with ¼" seam and right sides together. Press seams open to make a strip set. Make (2) strip sets.

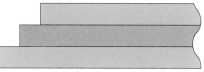

Make 2 strip sets

3. Lay out (2) 3" x WOF aqua strips and (2) 3" x WOF print strips as shown. Offset the strips by 3" at the top. Sew strips with ¼" seam and right sides together. Press seams open to make a strip set. Make (2) strip sets.

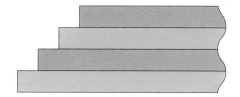

Make 2 strip sets

4. Lay the strip sets on a cutting mat. Use the 45-degree line on the mat or the 45-degree line on the ruler to cut 3"-wide strips at a 45-degree angle as shown. Cut 9 argyle strips from each strip set for a total of 36 argyle strips.

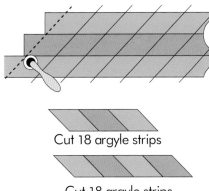

Cut 18 argyle strips

Cut 18 argyle strips

5. Lay out 4 argyle strips as shown. The strip sets from step 2 should be on the outside edges. Referring to the numbers on the diagram, flip strip set 2 onto strip set 1, right sides together. Check to be sure the seams will meet when sewn together with a ¼" seam. Pin the seam at each intersection. Sew the strip sets together and press the seam open. In the same manner, sew strip set 3 to strip set 2 and strip set 4 to strip set 3 to complete the A set. Press seams open. Make 9 A sets.

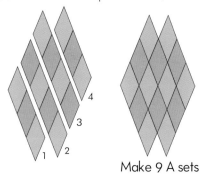

Make 9 A sets

6. Position an A set on a cutting mat as shown. Lay the QCR on the A set, lining up the 5" marking on the center diamonds. Trim at 5", along the right edge of the QCR. Lift the ruler and rotate the set 180-degrees. Position the ruler on the other side of the A set. Trim at 5", along the left edge of the QCR to make an A block. The A block should measure 10"-wide. Repeat with the remaining A sets to make 9 A blocks.

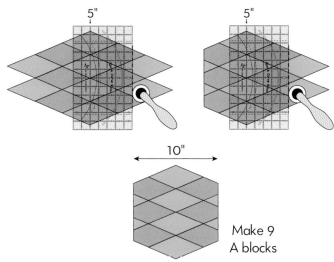

Make 9 A blocks

7. Position the QCR on an A block so the 6" intersection on the ruler is positioned on point 'x' as shown. Center the top and bottom of the block between the solid 1" and 11" lines of the ruler. Cut in the ruler's curve cut out. Lift the ruler and rotate the block 180-degrees. In the same manner, trim the opposite side of the block to make a curved A block. Make 9 curved A blocks.

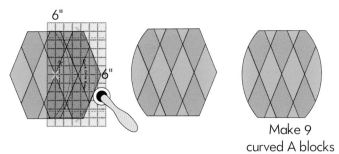

Make 9 curved A blocks

PIECING THE CURVES

1. Referring to the diagram, position a curved A block on B, right sides together, with a $\frac{1}{4}$" tail of B showing. Hold one piece in each hand and slowly bring the curved edges together while stitching a $\frac{1}{4}$" seam.

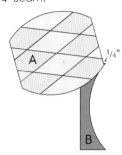
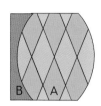

2. In the same manner, sew B to the opposite side of curved block A as shown. Press seams toward A to make a BAB shape. Make 9 BAB shapes.

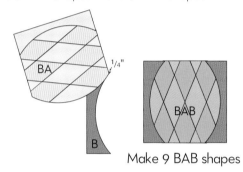

Make 9 BAB shapes

SQUARING UP THE SHAPES

Square up the BAB shapes to 9-$\frac{1}{2}$". Position a 10" or larger square-up ruler on BAB. Referring to the diagram, place the X at the 4-$\frac{3}{4}$" mark on the ruler. The curved seams at the top and bottom should be close to 2" and 7-$\frac{1}{2}$". Check to be sure there is approximately $\frac{1}{4}$" of gray background fabric on the sides. This will be your seam allowance when piecing the blocks together. Square up the remaining BAB shapes to make 9 argyle blocks.

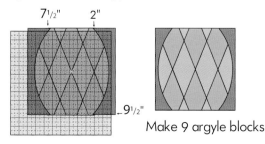

Make 9 argyle blocks

MAKING THE SASHING BLOCKS

1. Lay out (2) 4" x WOF strips and (1) 2-$\frac{1}{2}$" x WOF strip as shown. Sew the strips right sides together with $\frac{1}{4}$" seams. Press seams toward the white strip to make a strip set. Make 2 strip sets. From the strip sets, cut (12) 5" x 9-$\frac{1}{2}$" sashing blocks.

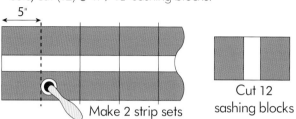

Make 2 strip sets

Cut 12 sashing blocks

2. Lay out (2) 4" x 20" gray strips and (1) 2-$\frac{1}{2}$" x 20" white strip as shown. Sew the strips right sides together and with $\frac{1}{4}$" seams. Press seams toward the white strip to make a strip set. From the strip set, cut (12) 3" x 9-$\frac{1}{2}$" sashing blocks.

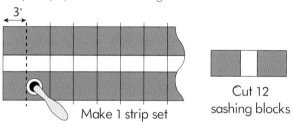

Make 1 strip set

Cut 12 sashing blocks

MAKING THE SASHING ROWS

1. Lay out the sashing blocks and gray squares and rectangles as shown. Sew the pieces right sides together with $\frac{1}{4}$" seams. Press seams to make a 3" x 41-$\frac{1}{2}$" sashing row. Make 2.

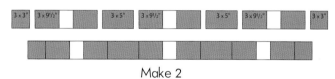

Make 2

2. Lay out the sashing blocks and gray squares and rectangles as shown. Sew the pieces right sides together with $\frac{1}{4}$" seams. Press seams to make a 5" x 41-$\frac{1}{2}$" sashing row. Make 2.

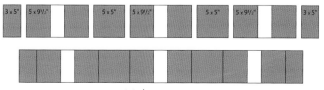

Make 2

MAKING THE BLOCK ROWS

Lay out the argyle blocks and sashing blocks as shown. Sew the blocks right sides together with ¼" seams. Press seams to make a 9-½" x 41-½" block row. Make 3 block rows.

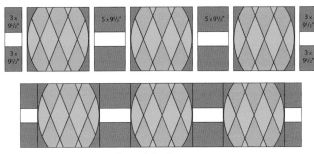

Make 3 block rows

QUILT ASSEMBLY

1. Referring to the Quilt Assembly Diagram, lay out the sashing rows and block rows as shown.

2. Sew the rows together to complete the quilt top. Press.

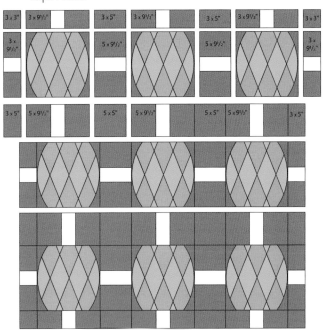

Quilt Assembly Diagram

FINISHING THE QUILT

1. Layer the quilt top, batting and backing together. Quilt as desired.

2. Sew the (5) 2-½" x WOF binding strips together to make one continuous strip. Press the strip in half lengthwise and sew the binding strip to the raw edge of the quilt top. Fold over raw edges and hand stitch in place on back of quilt.

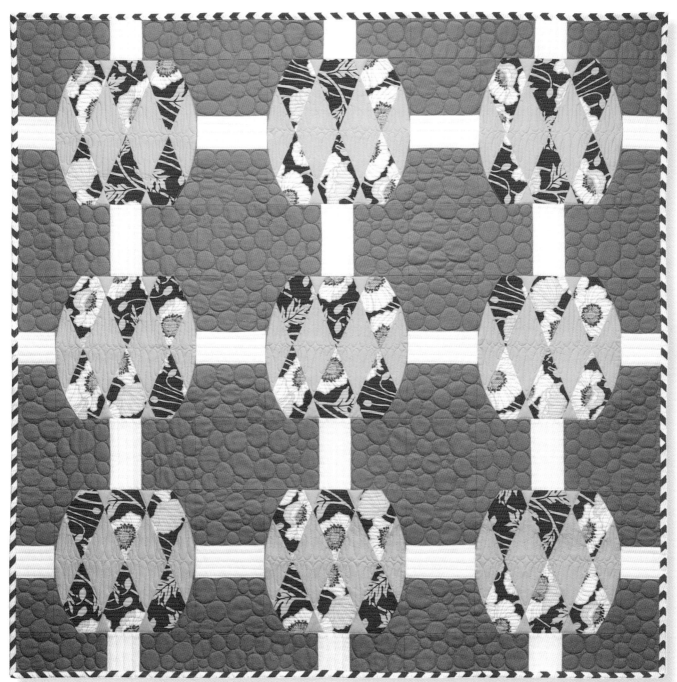

Finished size: 78" x 97"

Chic and Checkered

MATERIALS

⅓ yard each of 10 assorted solid color fabrics
2-½ yards white fabric
4 yards gray fabric
6 yards backing fabric
¾ yard binding fabric
Queen-size batting
Quick Curve Ruler© (QCR)

GENERAL CUTTING INSTRUCTIONS

From each assorted solid color fabric, cut:
(4) 2-½" x WOF strips. From the strips, cut:
    (8) 2-½" x 21" strips. (You will only use 7.)

From the white fabric, cut:
(35) 2-½" x WOF strips. From the strips, cut:
    (70) 2-½" x 21" strips.

From the gray fabric, cut:
Note: Fold the fabric in half lengthwise and refer to diagram before cutting the following squares and rectangles.
(12) 14-½" squares
(80) 3" x 10" rectangles

Fold
Length of fabric

| 3" x 10" |
| 3" x 10" |
| 14-1/2" square |

(4) 21-¾" squares. Cut each square in half twice on the diagonal to make 16 side setting triangles. (You will only use 14.)
(2) 11-⅛" squares. Cut each square in half once on the diagonal to make 4 corner triangles.

WOF = width of fabric
Read through Using the Quick Curve Ruler© on pages 6-9 before beginning this project.

MAKING THE BLOCK CENTERS

1. Lay out (4) 2-½" x 21" matching solid color strips and (3) 2-½" x 21" white strips as shown. Sew the strips together to make a strip set A. Press the seams in one direction. Make 1 strip set A with each solid color fabric for a total of 4 strip set A.

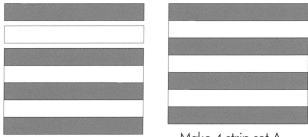

Make 4 strip set A

2. Lay out (4) 2-½" x 21" white strips and (3) 2-½" x 21" matching solid color strips as shown. Sew the strips together to make a strip set B. Press the seams in one direction. Make 1 strip set B with each solid color fabric for a total of 4 strip set B.

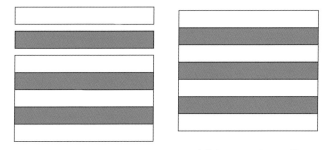

Make 4 strip set B

3. Referring to the diagrams, cut (8) 2-½" segments from each strip set A and (7) 2-½" segments from each strip set B.

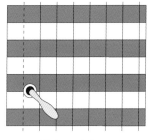

Strip set A
Cut 8 segments

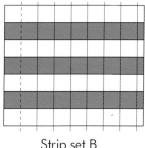

Strip set B
Cut 7 segments

4. Lay out (4) 2-½" A segments and (3) 2-½" B segments as shown. Sew the segments together to make a block center. Press the seams in opposite directions so the intersections will nest together. The block center should measure 14-½" square. Repeat with the remaining A and B segments to make a total of 20 block centers; 2 per solid color.

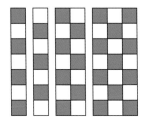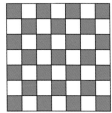

Make 20 block centers

CUTTING THE CURVES

1. Stack a few 3" x 10" gray rectangles vertically, right sides up. Position the QCR on the rectangles centering the top and bottom of the rectangles between the 1" and 11" lines. The right side of the fabric should be on the ruler's 1" vertical line as shown. Using a rotary cutter, cut in the ruler's curve cut out to make A shapes. Repeat with the remaining 3" x 10" gray rectangles to cut a total of 80 A shapes.

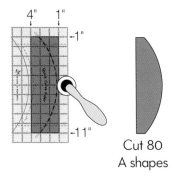

Cut 80
A shapes

2. Referring to the diagram, position the QCR over the left side of a block center with the left edge of the block on the ruler's 2-¾" vertical line. Center the

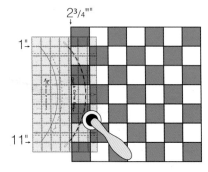

first and last horizontal seam of the block between the solid 1" and 11" lines of the ruler. Cut in the ruler's curve cut out. Repeat on the remaining 3 sides of the block center.

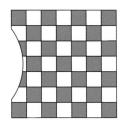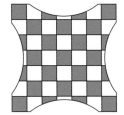

3. Cut curves on the remaining block centers.

PIECING THE CURVES

1. Referring to the diagram, position an A shape on one side of a block center, right sides together, with a ⅛" to ¼" of A extending over a curved side of the block center.

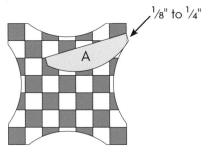

2. Hold one piece in each hand and slowly bring the curved edges together while stitching a ¼" seam. In the same manner, sew A shapes to the remaining 3 sides of the block center. Press seams away from the center to make a block. Make 20 blocks.

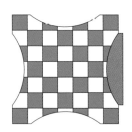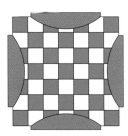

Make 20 blocks

SQUARING UP THE BLOCKS

Align the edge of the QCR along one side of the block. Trim any excess gray fabric to square up the side. Repeat on the remaining 3 sides. Square up all the blocks.

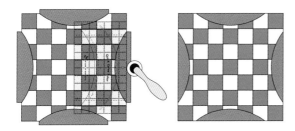

QUILT ASSEMBLY

1. Referring to the Quilt Top Assembly Diagram, lay out the 20 blocks, (12) 14-$\frac{1}{2}$" gray squares and 14 side setting triangles in diagonal rows as shown.

Quilt Top Assembly Diagram

2. Sew the pieces together in diagonal rows. Press the seams in each row in alternating directions.

3. Sew diagonal rows 1 through 4 together and rows 5 through 8 together. Press. Sew the sections together, pressing the seam open.

4. Sew a corner triangle to each corner to complete the quilt top.

5. Square up the quilt top, leaving $\frac{1}{4}$" beyond the block points.

FINISHING THE QUILT

1. Layer the quilt top, batting and backing together. Quilt as desired.

2. Sew the (9) 2-$\frac{1}{2}$" x WOF binding strips together to make one continuous strip. Press the strip in half lengthwise and sew the binding strip to the raw edge of the quilt top. Fold over raw edges and hand stitch in place on back of quilt.